WHEN STRAVINSKY MET NIJINSKY

Two Artists, Their Ballet, and One Extraordinary Riot

LAUREN STRINGER

HARCOURT CHILDREN'S BOOKS

Houghton Mifflin Harcourt

Boston New York 2013

When Stravinsky composed music all by himself,
his piano trilled an orchestra
with violins and flutes, trumpets and tubas,
and kettledrums that lightly pom-di-di-pommed
with the ringling and tingling of cymbals and bells.

But he dreamed of making something different and new.

When Nijinsky composed dances all by himself,
his torso floated—a swan. His legs leaped—a deer!
And his feet, like a sparrow, tippy-tip-toed,
while his arms curved and swerved like a snake.

But he dreamed of making something different and new.

Then Stravinsky met Nijinsky
and his music began to change.

His piano pirouetted a puppet,
his tuba leaped a loping bear,
and his trumpet tah-tahed
a twirling ballerina.

And when Nijinsky met Stravinsky,
his dance began to change.

His torso trumpeted a melody,

his arms and legs sang from strings,
and his feet began
to pom-di-di-pom like timpani.

Stravinsky inspired Nijinsky.
Nijinsky inspired Stravinsky.

Together they decided to dream of something different and new.

Stravinsky said, "Nijinsky,
let's remember our old home, Russia.
Perhaps from the old will come something new?
I'll play a deep forest where dancers can leap.
They'll need night drums that rumble and fires that blaze."

And Nijinsky said, "Yes! They will jump 'round in circles
and their feet must be muddy!
Can you make a mud sound?"

So they took Russian folk dances and Russian folk songs,

they squared them and flattened them, twisted and cubed them,

turning them into something different and new!

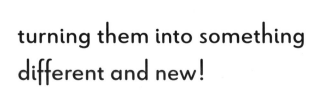

At rehearsal,
some of the dancers
declared it a mess
and one or two
musicians walked out.
But enough of them stayed
and enough of them played,
drumming their feet and beating their drums
to rollicking chords and rhythms offbeat.

And when it was ready . . .

Stravinsky and Nijinsky
brought their new show to town.

The night began sweetly with a single bassoon.

Then it grew . . .

The dancers stomped and skipped and jumped—
"They're not dancing the way dancers should dance!"

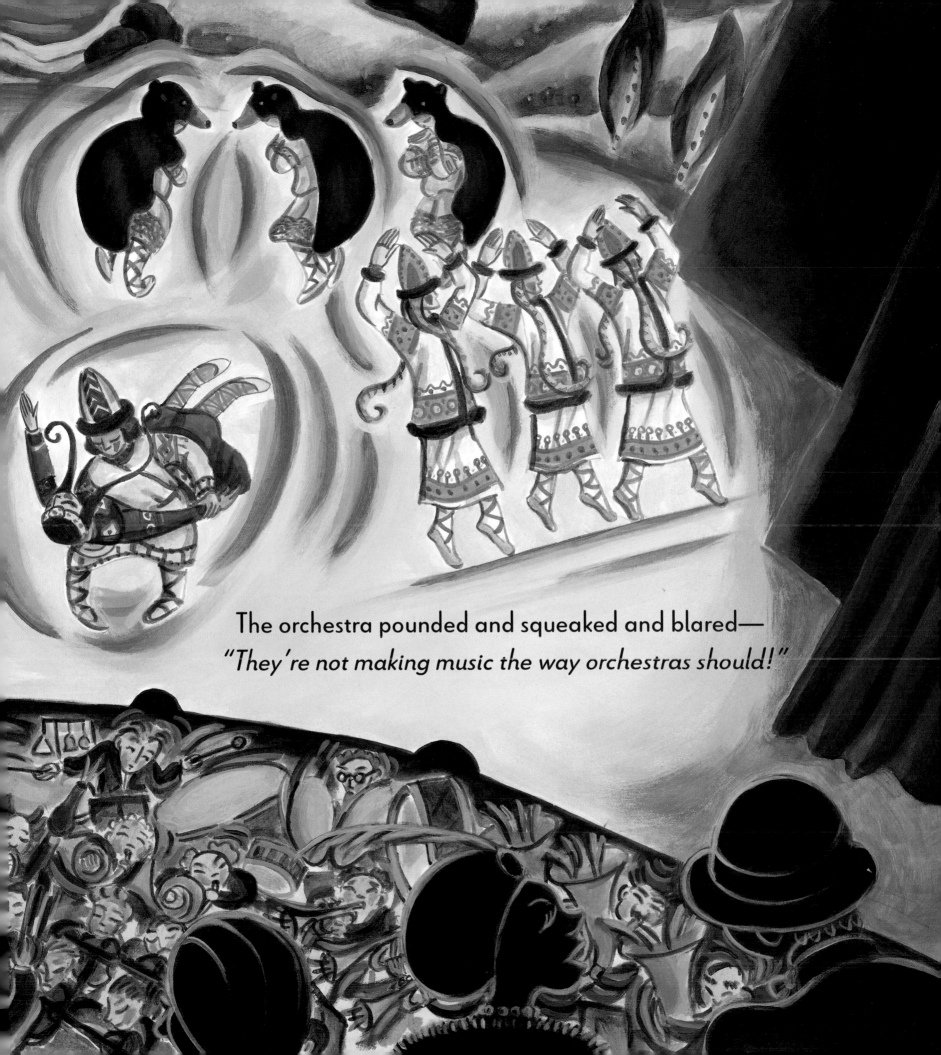

The orchestra pounded and squeaked and blared—
"They're not making music the way orchestras should!"

Some people hated it! They were nettled by the new.
They stood on their seats and shouted: **"Boo! Boo! Boo!"**
They threw hats and hairpins, gloves and boots;
they pounded their fists and stamped their feet.

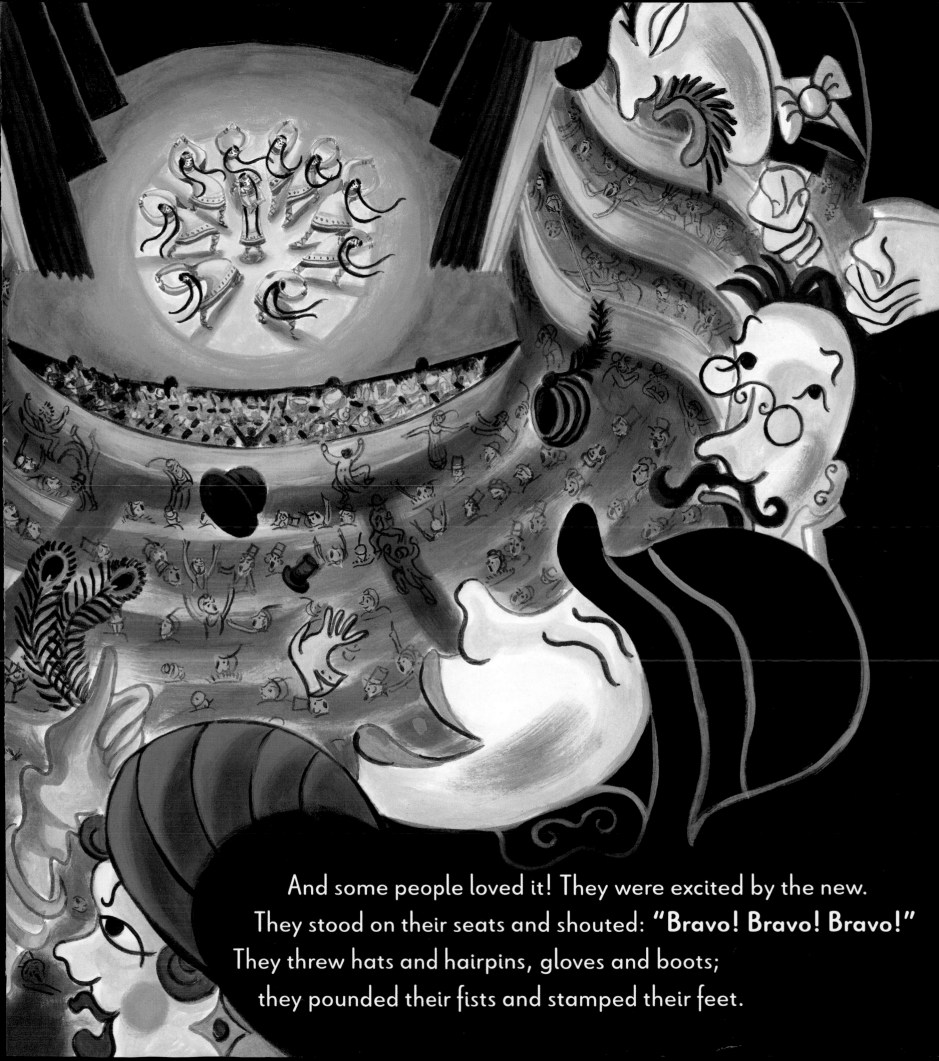

And some people loved it! They were excited by the new.
They stood on their seats and shouted: "Bravo! Bravo! Bravo!"
They threw hats and hairpins, gloves and boots;
they pounded their fists and stamped their feet.

The crowd poured into the street when the curtain went down,
rioting and bellowing, buzzing and hurdling,
wild with the night that brought something brand-new!

When Stravinsky met Nijinsky after the show,
he said, "Nijinsky, what a ruckus we made tonight!"
And Nijinsky said, "What an uproar and what a delight!
Will music and dance ever be the same?"
Then they smiled and they laughed and they both agreed—

something *very* different and new began this remarkable night.

A NOTE FROM THE AUTHOR

Leafing through the program while waiting for the hall to dim and the Minnesota Orchestra to begin, I was struck by a photograph of two men, one dressed in tux and tails and the other costumed like a sad clown. When I read who they were, Stravinsky and Nijinsky, I loved the rhythm and rhyme of their names. I was amazed to learn that the ballet they collaborated on, *The Rite of Spring,* had revolutionized the world of music and dance. I had to know more. My research led me to the riot in Paris the night of the ballet's premiere. It impressed me deeply that art could make such an impact that people would begin yelling and fighting in the aisles. Was it the realization that they were watching the world of music and dance change before them? Would I have accepted something so different and new had I been at the Théâtre des Champs-Élysées on that fateful night? Artists often create new ways of seeing, hearing, and experiencing the world, and that is just what Stravinsky and Nijinsky did. Together they created a ballet like no other of its time.

IGOR STRAVINSKY (1882–1971)

Igor Stravinsky is one of the most important and influential composers of modern music of the twentieth century. When he was eight years old, he was mesmerized by a performance of Tchaikovsky's *Sleeping Beauty* at the Mariinsky Theatre in Russia. After this pivotal experience he began piano lessons and studied music theory in earnest, but when he grew older his father insisted he study law instead. His father died in 1902, and Stravinsky returned to music, studying with the Russian composer Rimsky-Korsakov. Stravinsky used the piano to compose music for a full orchestra, having the keen ability to hear the sounds of many different instruments in his imagination. When one of Stravinsky's early compositions, *Fireworks,* was first performed, it was heard by the impresario of the Ballets Russes, Sergei Diaghilev, who invited Stravinsky to compose music for his new ballet *The Firebird.* This would be Stravinsky's first ballet. Its unusual rhythms and dissonant melodies, so different from the more harmonious music of the nineteenth century, excited the chic Parisian audience. In 1911, he met Nijinsky while writing music for the ballet *Petrushka.* Again, Stravinsky's music was a success, as was Nijinsky's interpretation of the music when he danced as the puppet Petrushka. Stravinsky and Nijinsky became an inspired and inspiring team. When *The Rite of Spring* premiered in 1913, Stravinsky was thrust to the forefront of modern music. Throughout his long life he composed music that to this day inspires composers, choreographers, visual artists, and writers.

Igor Stravinsky and Vaslav Nijinsky
as Petrushka in 1911

VASLAV NIJINSKY (1889–1950)

Vaslav Nijinsky is celebrated as the greatest male dancer of the twentieth century. As a young child, he performed all over Russia with his parents' dance company. When Nijinsky was nine, his mother enrolled him in classes at the Imperial School of Ballet in Saint Petersburg. Because of his grand leaps that seemed to defy gravity and his ability to dance *en pointe,* or on the tips of the toes, an unusual skill for a male dancer, Nijinsky stood out. When he joined Sergei Diaghilev and the Ballets Russes, Nijinsky became an instant sensation in Europe. His performance as the lovelorn puppet Petrushka in Stravinsky's ballet of the same name was such a success that Diaghilev made certain that Nijinsky worked with Stravinsky on *The Rite of Spring,* this time in the role of choreographer. Nijinsky's choreography for *The Rite of Spring* was accused of "crimes against beauty and grace" by some, yet this pivotal work has inspired dancers and choreographers since its premiere.

THE RITE OF SPRING

By the time the *The Rite of Spring,* or *Le sacre du printemps,* was first performed at the Théâtre des Champs-Élysées on May 29, 1913, by the Ballets Russes, forty-six dancers and ninety-nine orchestra members had met for more than one hundred rehearsals. But in only thirty-four minutes, the world of music and dance was shocked and changed forever. Almost as soon as the piece began, the extraordinarily high notes of the bassoon were so unfamiliar to the audience that many began to laugh or boo. Influenced by the Russian folk songs of his youth, Stravinsky had written music in higher registers that made the instruments sound like untrained village voices. When the dancers entered the stage jumping heavily up and down using gestures inspired by Russian folk dances, their

Dancers in *The Rite of Spring* in 1913

feet intentionally turned inward, the protests in the theater grew louder. The audience was used to the long, graceful lines of traditional ballets such as *Swan Lake* or *The Nutcracker.* Arguments sprang up between supporters and opponents of the work, followed by shouts and fistfights in the aisles. The unrest escalated into a riot and the police were called in.

The Paris music critic for the *New York Times,* Carl Van Vechten, was shocked when a young man behind him began drumming his fists on Van Vechten's head! From his memoirs of the premiere, Stravinsky wrote, "I stood in the wings behind Nijinsky holding his coattails, while he stood on a chair shouting numbers to the dancers." With all the noise in the audience, the dancers could barely keep track of the beats. In the end there were four or five curtain calls, all of the artists receiving both vigorous applause and vigorous protests. But no matter which side they were on, everyone there witnessed the birth of modern music and modern dance.

ABOUT THE ILLUSTRATIONS

Dance and music were not the only arts undergoing colossal change at the beginning of the twentieth century. All of the arts were exploding in new compositions, colors, and dimensions. In celebration of that change, I have made reference to many of my favorite paintings from that time throughout this book. To illustrate when Stravinsky and Nijinsky first met in 1911, I found inspiration in elements from *The Red Studio* by Henri Matisse, painted in the same year. Cubism took the art world by storm in 1907 when Pablo Picasso painted *Les Desmoiselles d'Avignon.* Several of my illustrations reflect the cubist influence on the angular, flattened choreography of Nijinsky and the fractured, dissonant chords of Stravinsky's music. I painted patterns on curtains, furniture, and clothing based on works by Matisse and designs by Léon Bakst, set and costume designer for the Ballets Russes. It was the set and costume designer for *The Rite of Spring,* Nicholas Roerich, whose knowledge and research of ancient Russian cultures inspired Stravinsky and Nijinsky. In my illustration of the ballet's first rehearsal, Roerich is sketching bear costumes beside the founder of the Ballets Russes, Sergei Diaghilev. The conductor Pierre Monteux is featured in my illustrations of the orchestra playing *The Rite of Spring.* Despite the hubbub going on around him, he conducted Stravinsky's score from beginning to end without missing a beat.

For teachers in the arts, who nurture the imaginations of young
artists everywhere, and for M., R., and C. with awe and love

Acknowledgments

There are several people who deserve loud applause for their help with this book. Bravo! to Anne Ylvisaker, Kaye Denny,
Catherine Thimmesh, KTM, and Cooper Smith. Bravo! to my editor Samantha McFerrin and designer Elizabeth Tardiff for their
unflagging enthusiasm and excellent suggestions. Bravo! with gratitude to the Loft Literary Center and to the McKnight Foundation
for their enormous support of writers, artists, and this manuscript. And a very loud Bravo! to the magnificent contributions
and encouragement from my husband—best friend, composer, and author—Matthew Smith.

Sources

Berg, Shelley C. Le Sacre du printemps: *Seven Productions from Nijinsky to Martha Graham.* Ann Arbor: UMI Research Press, 1988.

Bowlt, John E., Zelfira Tregulova, and Nathalie Rosticher Giordano. *A Feast of Wonders: Sergei Diaghilev and the Ballets Russes.* Milano: Skira, 2009.

Eksteins, Modris. *Rites of Spring: The Great War and the Birth of the Modern Age.* Boston: Houghton Mifflin, 1989.

Kelly, Thomas Forrest. *First Nights: Five Musical Premieres.* New Haven: Yale University Press, 2000.

Kelly, Thomas Forrest. Harvard Great Teachers: "On Stravinsky." Website: www.greatteachers.harvard.edu/videos/thomas-kelly-stravinsky.

Marsh, Geoffrey, Jane Pritchard, and Sarah Sonner. *Diaghilev and the Golden Age of the Ballets Russes: 1909–1929.*
London: Victoria and Albert Museum, 2011.

Thomas, Michael Tilson. *Keeping Score:* "Stravinsky's *The Rite of Spring.*" PBS. Website: www.pbs.org/keepingscore/stravinsky-rite-of-spring.html.

The text in this book was set in Le Havre Rounded.
The illustrations were done in acrylic on Arches 140 lb. watercolor paper.
The display type was set in Larisch.

Library of Congress Cataloging-in-Publication Data
Stringer, Lauren.
When Stravinsky met Nijinsky : two artists, their ballet, and one extraordinary riot / Lauren Stringer.
ISBN 978-0-547-90725-3
1. Stravinsky, Igor, 1882–1971 Ballets—Juvenile literature. 2. Nijinsky, Waslaw, 1890–1950—Juvenile literature. I. Title.
ML3930.S86S77 2013
781.5'56092—dc23
2012025330

Manufactured in China
SCP 10 9 8 7 6 5 4 3 2 1
4500388531